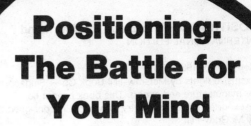

Positioning:
The Battle for
Your Mind

First Edition—revised
by
Al Ries, Chairman
Trout & Ries, Inc.
and
Jack Trout, President
Trout & Ries, Inc.

McGraw-Hill Book Company

New York St. Louis San Francisco Auckland Bogotá
Hamburg Johannesburg London Madrid Mexico
Montreal New Delhi Panama Paris São Paulo
Singapore Sydney Tokyo Toronto

POSITIONING: The Battle for Your Mind
INTERNATIONAL EDITION

This book was set in New Baskerville by University Graphics, Inc.
The editors were William A. Sabin and Jim Bessent
The production supervisor was Thomas G. Kowalczyk.

Library of Congress Cataloging in Publication Data

Ries, Al.
    Positioning; the battle for your mind.

    Includes index.
    1. Positioning (Advertising) I. Troute, Jack.
II. Title.
HF5827.2.R53 1986 659.1 85-14898
ISBN 0-07-065264-3

When ordering this title use ISBN 0-07-100273-1

PRINTED AND BOUND BY B & JO ENTERPRISE PTE LTD, SINGAPORE.

**Dedicated to the second best
advertising agency in the whole world.**

Whoever they might be.

Chapter 13. When Line Extension Can Work

There are cases, however, of successful line extension (GE, for example.) A discussion of when to use the house name and when to use a new name. 115

Chapter 14. Positioning a Company: Xerox

Xerox owns the copier position. But as Xerox moves into the office automation field, how should the company be positioned? . .127

Chapter 15. Positioning a Country: Belgium

The answer to the problems of a national airline like Sabena Belgium World Airlines is to position the country, not the airline. 137

Chapter 16. Positioning an Island: Jamaica

"Sand and surf" has become a visual cliché for all Caribbean islands. How do you establish a unique position for one of them? 143

Chapter 17. Positioning a Product: Milk Duds

How a product with a small budget can get into the mind by positioning itself as the long-lasting alternative to the candy bar. .149

Chapter 18. Positioning a Service: Mailgram

Why a totally new service has to be positioned against the old. 153

Chapter 19. Positioning a Long Island Bank

How a bank successfully struck back when its territory was invaded by its giant neighbors from the Big City. 159

Chapter 20. Positioning a New Jersey Bank

One of the best ways to establish a position is to find a weakness in your competitor's. 167

Chapter 21. Positioning a ski resort: Stowe

How an outside expert can add credibility to a positioning claim. 173

Chapter 22. Positioning the Catholic Church

Even institutions can benefit from positioning thinking. An outline of the logical steps that could be taken to position the Roman Catholic Church. 177

Chapter 23. Positioning Yourself and Your Career

You can benefit by using positioning strategy to advance your own career. Key principle: Don't try to do everything yourself. Find a horse to ride. 183

Chapter 24. Positioning Your Business

To get started on a positioning program, there are six questions you can ask yourself. 193

Chapter 25. Playing the Positioning Game

To be successful at positioning, you have to have the right mental attitude. You have to become an outside-in thinker rather than an inside-out thinker. This requires patience, courage, and strength of character. 201

Index 211

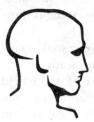

Introduction

"What we have here is a failure to communicate."

How often have you heard that bromide? "Failure to communicate" is the single, most common, most universal reason people give for their problems.

Business problems, government problems, labor problems, marriage problems.

If only people took the time to communicate their feelings, to explain their reasons, the assumption is that many of the problems of the world would somehow disappear. People seem to believe any problem can be solved if only the parties sit down and talk.

Unlikely.

Today, communication itself is the problem. We have become the world's first overcommunicated society. Each year, we send more and receive less.

A new approach to communication

This book has been written about a new approach to communication called *positioning*. And most of the examples are from the most difficult of all forms of communication—advertising. A form of communication that, from the point of view of the recipient, is held in low esteem. Advertising is, for the most part, unwanted and unliked. In some cases, advertising is thoroughly detested.

To many intellectuals, advertising is selling your soul to corporate America—a subject not worthy of serious study.

In spite of its reputation, or perhaps because of it, the field of advertising is a superb testing ground for theories of communication. If it works in advertising, most likely it will work in politics, religion, or any other activity that requires mass communication.

So the examples in this book could just as well have been taken from the field of politics, war, business, or even the science of chasing the opposite sex. Or any form of human activity which involves influencing the minds of other people. Whether you want to promote a car, a cola, a computer, a candidate, or your own career.

Positioning is a concept that has changed the nature of advertising, a concept so simple, people have difficulty understanding how powerful it is.

Every successful politician practices positioning. So do Procter & Gamble and Johnson & Johnson.

Positioning defined

Positioning starts with a product. A piece of merchandise, a service, a company, an institution, or even a person. Perhaps yourself.

But positioning is not what you do to a product. Positioning is what you do to the mind of the prospect. That is, you position the product in the mind of the prospect.

So it's incorrect to call the concept "product positioning." You're not really doing something to the product itself.

Not that positioning doesn't involve change. It often does. But changes made in the name, the price, and the package are really not changes in the product at all. They're basically cosmetic changes done for the purpose of securing a worthwhile position in the prospect's mind.